WALTER PISTON

DUO

for Viola and Violoncello

AMP-8079

Associated Music Publishers, Inc.

DISTRIBUTED BY
HAL•LEONARD® CORPORATION
7777 W. BLUEMOUND RD. P.O. BOX 13819 MILWAUKEE, WI 53213

to Sven and Kurt Reher

DUO

I

Walter Piston

Viola

II

III

WALTER PISTON

DUO
for Viola and Violoncello

AMP-8079

Associated Music Publishers, Inc.

DISTRIBUTED BY
HAL•LEONARD®
CORPORATION
7777 W. BLUEMOUND RD. P.O. BOX 13819 MILWAUKEE, WI 53213

to Sven and Kurt Reher

DUO
I

Walter Piston

II

Andante sereno ♪= 96

8

III

Allegro brillante ♩= 126.

Belmont Mass.

Belmont Mass.